The Eyes

of

God

J James

ISBN 979-8-89043-459-3 (paperback)
ISBN 979-8-89043-460-9 (digital)

Christian Faith Publishing
832 Park Avenue
Meadville, PA 16335
www.christianfaithpublishing.com

Printed in the United States of America

To Verna Lewis

Introduction

Life is like a meandering river, a path with many forks, and we have the choices to either stop at the next bend or travel to the left or right path. We do not know what the future holds, but only that, what we choose in life will have a lasting effect. We may not see the results of ours or other's actions, but rest assured, they will show themselves. So it is with my life. There were still many paths to follow, but before I chose which direction I would go, I reflected many times on events long past that affected me for my lifetime. I believe God created us all for a purpose, no matter how insignificant we may feel those purposes are. He created all things for a purpose. Not just things but events, seasons, times, and oh yes, incredibly special people.

I am educated as a biologist. I worked as a creator and designer, and I have held most precious the desire to teach and learn. Today I am retired and reflecting on my life. The Lord is our master teacher, and those lessons he teaches us, prepare us, remind us of his grace, and instill in us a desire to know him more deeply. And when we honestly seek Him, *honestly* seek Him, he reveals himself in all his creation. He also does not forget us nor forsake us. He is always there and always readying to reveal himself if we want to know him. Sometimes he reveals himself through people or events, but the lessons he teaches are lasting. The lessons we learn are indelibly marked in our lives, hearts, and mind.

My hope is to convey a story of an incredibly special person whom the Lord used to change my life forever. To share about her and how the Lord used her is the greatest honor that I can give and give the Lord glory. As my life has meandered, I often reflect on those times and people who have made the most lasting impression on me, my walk with God, and my relationships with others. As I have grown older and as yet to be wiser, her memory shines vividly within me. I will not forget her. I will not put aside the lessons I learned. I will not stop striving to reach for the love that she was able to display. I will not fail the Lord to honor Him through her story. I will not allow her memory to disappear.

Although this story is about a young girl named Verna, the implications are for how she changed my life and the lives of those I have interacted with over these many years. How the Lord allowed her to impact many facets of who I am today is the theme of this writing, and therefore, the focal point will be my life. Without that foundation, the reality of who this wonderful girl was, how she shared a special life, and how God used her would be meaningless. A rare gift by any standard is precious, and Verna was a rare gift.

Now, as a much older man whom the Lord has blessed with many opportunities, and chastened for my falling away, much as so many of us may have done, I reflect on the start of my meandering path of life and faith in Jesus Christ. He has never forsaken me but has trained me up so I may not fall away and serve Him in my later years. The Holy Spirit uses so many events in our lives, and our path is directed by our conscious desire to listen to that "still small voice" and be in tune with the Lord and Savior of our souls and in this case, my case, the interactions of others. Things have not always gone as I wanted them, as a very selfish person, but that does not mean our will cannot be aligned with His will.

So as I share this life story, I pray you will be able to glean some God-given wisdom from my mistakes, corrections, and downright foolish actions to gain perhaps some insights and ways to not stumble over the pitfalls of life and have a more joy-filled life by following the Lord and His ways for our lives.

I meet people all over the United States. My past occupations often had me traveling and at times striking up conversations while waiting for a plane, having a meal, or in line for some dutiful responsibility like an ATM. People all share a common trait. We all have some event or person in our lives that we can reflect on. Sometimes those memories were good, and sometimes they cause the very hair of our neck to stand on edge with fear or anger.

Nevertheless, they affect us. It was during one of these conversations that a young waitress reminded me of this special time in my life. I did a lot of travel, and when I had stopped at a small town and was having dinner, this waitress appeared to be rather tall. I asked her what her height was, and she shared with me she was six feet, six inches. Of course, I suggested she may have played basketball or volleyball in high school. But I was surprised to learn from our discussion that she was on a Semi-Pro Hockey team and had been selected to play on that famous women's Olympic hockey team that took gold in the winter Olympics. As she was readying herself to travel to Finland for the team preparation, she was contacted about her mother. She relinquished that dream to stay beside her mother while she died of cancer. What a sacrifice of love. I have often reflected, but this time, she looked into me with something in her eyes, a look that brought that past time in my life to vivid detail and reminded me. My life had become so busy, so successful, I had almost forgotten.

Children grow up. Well, some do. When I returned home after one of my lengthy battles with airports, bus stops, and train stations, my wonderful wife greeted me. She is never without words of wisdom that inspire me to consider very deeply what my life has to offer God and others. I often feel I have failed the Lord in His service.

My prayer is to share this short story openly, honestly, and without betrayal to Verna. My prayer is that God may use me to bring Him glory and her life the honor she deserves. Until now, I have never shared with anyone what happened to me and how it started the change of who I am. I held these events very close and tight, not allowing anyone to even get a small glimpse of who I really may be. This is a me that only God knows. I am still not done and will never be done growing into that person I prayed I wanted to be when I was a young boy growing up in Alaska. I only hope I can do justice to this beautiful person I remember. She showed me love, forgiveness, and sacrifice through her life, through her eyes, and as I looked into them, they gave me a glimpse into the Eyes of God.

Chapter One

A Look Back

Change is good. But good change is even better. We do not always view life from a perspective that we must change in order to live. In fact, God is our greatest agent of change, and if we allow Him, we will be changed or transformed into a person who will be more like the living God who created us. Dare we ask Him to change us to be more like Him?

I love the autumn. I love the seasons, and I suppose we all have seasons in our lives. I am in one of those seasons now, a time of reflection and evaluation. We call it later life, but I wish that I were at the start of my life. Then I would have so much more time to use the wisdom that we all collect over the years. I suppose there is still much time to use the many lessons we learn. We just do not always think on these things as we should.

Sometimes I sit quietly and ask the Lord what he has in mind for me. Can this be all? The wind blows the leaves, and the chill of the autumn air sneaks through the cracks in the window to touch my soul. Why is the autumn so beautiful, and yet it is the start of a time so cold and dark? That always fascinated me. How there can be such beauty for such a short time just before what appears, on the surface, to be death?

The leaves fall; the trees look silently into dark skies like majestic sentinels waiting for a better time. Perhaps, these are simple signs and reminders for us and our lives. We blossom into this world, grow strong and full of life, and then for a brief moment in time, we may shine with glorious color and then pass into darkness to await a time in the future when we will all blossom again, anew, forever.

I suppose that is why this season of year brings deep reflection. I was seven years old when my father was offered a job with a pulp mill in Sitka, Alaska. We were a family of five children, my older brother, my two younger sisters, and a baby brother of only a few months old. I was number 2 of what would later be a total of six children. We, the five of us, were all to accompany our arrival to the brand-new forty-ninth state. The final addition, a miraculous gift from the Lord, would arrive two years later. That brother would complete my parent's nest of six children.

Moving to a whole new state, new life, new culture is, I am quite sure, a tremendous stress to anyone, especially a family of seven and most assuredly my father and mother. My dad went ahead of us to establish a house, his job, and with the community at large. This was to make our infusion into the *new world* an easier task. For my older brother and me, this was just a mere new adventure, not something to be feared or stressed over. Of course, we would hunt bears, make igloos, trap and fish, living off the land—Alaska, the great frontier. We were ready, and upon arrival, my father presented us with our first hunting knives to be immediately strapped to our belts on our hips and never to be removed. Mom was sure always to bring us back down to earth, and my two younger sisters were to knock lasting sense into me. At seven, in Alaska and on this adventure, the last thing I was thinking about was God. And yet, this indeed was God's country. This would also be the start of my spiritual adventure, and the course was set for me to begin viewing life through His eyes.

My reflections today during autumn, I am sure were no mistakes. Sort of preparations for which the Lord can grab hold of me and remind me. We all have those special times or smells, the sight or sounds that stir a feeling or desire. We call it nostalgia. I call it a gentle tapping on the shoulder of our lives from God. A way he gets our memory. A way he holds our attention, even if for only a moment, but nonetheless, he has our attention. We stop, we reflect, we for a moment can hear that still small voice. Now we must choose to listen.

We arrived in that small town, Sitka, on a gloomy, wet, drizzly October day. This is typical, I was to learn, of the weather in the southeast. Lots of rain, lots of clouds, lots of wet days. But we came from the dessert, so for me, no big deal, something new. We called it liquid sunshine, and we were drenched in it one hundred inches a year. This was not taking into consideration the snowfall as well. Oh yes, the snow was in addition to the rain. Nonetheless, the country was magnificent and held me in its grasp. I was instantly captured by the majestic grandeur of this world. Surely God's throne must reside somewhere in the mountains of such a beautiful realm.

Having a knowledge and sense of God was a part of our lives. My father had the greatest impact on me. His parents are from the *old country* of Hungary and from the East Coast. They came through Ellis Island and brought with them the customs of the Byzantine Church. I was raised Eastern Orthodox, Byzantine Catholic. So I was raised with all the pomp and culture of a Jewish temple, and to this day, I am filled with reverence to worship the

Lord in this manner. I look back today and see where my desire to know the Lord originated. Still, as a young boy, I did not know how the Lord would teach me to seek him.

I remember my father telling us as children, "You will not read the Sunday comics until after you go to church. Church comes first, God comes first." Of course, we as kids were always frustrated by his "rules." He was an amazingly simple man (he died of a massive heart attack at almost eighty-two) in the sense that he always taught us that God will take care of us. "He will always take care of you. Don't worry for tomorrow," he would say. He was always right because as we grew up and we were a typical lower middle-class family, we never had a lot, but we never were without. I believe now he gave me a strong foundation. But let me save that for later.

My mother (she recently died at an age over ninety years old) was a Lutheran in religious upbringing, and as a Protestant, she was most inclined to tell the gospel story and not as encased in religious ritual. Her parents came from Denmark, pre-World War II, and avoided the Nazi invasions and devastation of war. It was my mother who gave me my first small New Testament, Psalms, and Proverbs at age six on November 9, 1959, where I signed the "My Decision to Receive Christ as My Savior" in the back of the tiny book. I later was to give this to my youngest brother. I recently found it in some old "stuff." Later at the age of nine, she gave me a larger King James zip-up Bible with my name embossed on it, which sits by my bedside to this day. She was an encouragement to my spiritual growth.

At the age of seven, I did not consider what the future would hold or how I was to live it out. We just "lived." Arriving in October gave me an early chance to see the glorious land of many wonders, and of course, school was still fresh in the New Year. The excitement of meeting new friends was lifting my adventurous spirit. My mother always said that my father's Hungarian gypsy spirit was in our blood. I believe that to be true since even today, I enjoy going to new places, seeing new things, and above all, meeting new people. I was blessed with adventurous parents, and they allowed us to enjoy the wonder of God's creation.

Now, looking back at this point, I am reminded of the type of person I was at that time. I have not profoundly changed but only have learned that this, my personal temperament, still needs taming, to be placed in God's merciful and tender hands. I have always been self-sufficient and independent. I was tough and quite capable of taking care of myself. No one need worry about me because I would always be able to worry well enough on my own. I needed no one, no one, not even an all-powerful God, who is the creator of my very soul. Little did I realize how much I did need Him, and as time was to meander its way through the pages of my life, I reflect on just how much He was in control and how much I was not. Oh, how I wish now that I had had eyes that could see and ears that could hear. Oh, how I wish today that my self-sufficient, "I do not need anyone," "I have all the answers" attitude had been challenged and changed much sooner. But then, our God is a personal God who deals with us all in our own place, at our own time, and in His timing.

Although there was a desire to serve others, there was also a need to place myself first. Interestingly, the two words that define our behaviors are *desire* and *need*. If only I would have been able to discern the difference and how the Lord defined them in light of Himself and Jesus.

My family consisted of my older brother, myself often referred to as number 2, my sisters, and then later two younger brothers. I remember how my older brother was always my parent's first joy. My father, being very rooted in traditions, gave great value to the firstborn son. When my sister was born, she became the center of attention because she was the first girl, and then the next daughter came into this world, and she was, for several years, the baby. The next son was born, and he was always considered my mom's "Tiny Tim," her dream child, as she tells the story of a dream that she would someday have a child with curly blond hair. In fact, my younger brother (I am eight years older than he) had curly blond hair and was mistaken many times for a little girl, so it was clear his status in the family was established by my mother's special place for him.

Finally, my youngest brother arrived with fanfare and flair. He was our miracle baby, having been born in my mom's middle years and being delivered under very harsh circumstances. Not only was he a breach birth but the umbilical cord was wrapped around his neck. To complicate the delivery, my mother lost her water one week prior to his birth, and the doctor and nurse in this small Alaskan town of only three thousand had never before delivered such a difficult birth. He survived and became a wonderfully creative person, my mother's most precious gift and later in life to be my father's greatest heartache, for he was so special to my father. He was the fourth son of a fourth son.

I share this background for the purpose of giving insight into a personal perception of my status in the family and offer as an explanation, not an excuse, for my future behaviors. This is neither good nor bad as in any sibling and family situation but does impact our views on who and what we are in relation to our world. So these first formative years were to form who I would become and why this special encounter with a, I believe now, loving godsent person, would reform and remind me through my life who I really was in God's eyes.

The Bible is rich with the stories of family, parent and sibling relationships, and how they may have shaped the choices and manner in which the Lord must deal with us individually and collectively. Abraham was instructed to leave his family and go into the land that the Lord would show him. Instead, he delayed his departure until his father died and then proceeded to take along his nephew Lott against the Lord's instructions. We are always reminded of Cain and Able and the jealousy that turned into murder. Sin was crouching at Cain's heart. Isaac's family had favoritism with Esau and Jacob that resulted in deception and separation from each other, and of course, the jealousy of the brothers of Joseph sent a young boy into slavery in Egypt. They meant it for evil; God meant it for good (Genesis 50:20). The Lord knows the intentions of man's heart and "And we know that *all things work together for good* to them that *love God*, to them who are the called according to his purpose"(Romans 8:28). However, in all these things, God redeemed the circumstances, and in all cases, we find that God used these men in spite of their frailties, sinful nature, familial intervention, and personal drama. God knew what He had created and the need for a plan to redeem man out of his nature. The Bible, the written Word of God, outlines and details God's plan of salvation as part of His creation.

So it has been with me. These reflections only serve to remind me of His redemption, and I pray His preparation of my heart for His glory. Therefore, these looks back serve to foreshadow how the Lord must have dealt with my spirit and thereby open the chapter of my life that would forever change who I am in spite of myself. I needed these lessons to help guide my life in the future. Sometimes the Lord needs to chasten us in love, to show us how much we need Him. I always found it interesting that Jesus, when he met with Sal (later to be known as Paul), he blinded him so he could only focus on the words of Jesus, with full attention to what He would say to him and He uses this statement: Sal, Sal, why do you kick against the goad? The ox-goad is a long pole or stick with a pointed piece of iron fastened to one end. In the strong hands of a loving master, the ox is gently prodded, guided, steered, and driven in the desired direction when plowing the fields. When a stubborn ox attempts to kick back against the goad that is causing it discomfort, the ox will actually inflict more pain, driving the pointed end deeper into its flesh.

The goad was used only on oxen. Oxen were designed to serve the master. Christ was saying he created

Sal to serve the Lord, and he needed to yield to the master. Guess what? This is the lesson I was to learn later and throughout my life. I was created to serve the Risen Lord Jesus, not myself!

We lived in what I now refer to as an Alaskan paradise for over seven years. Each day, each hour was to be the most concentrated memories of my life. In the winter, we ice-skated on our frozen lake, sledded on "Bunker Hill," and enjoyed the wonderful holidays that only the seasons can bring, brightened by the northern lights. In the summer, when the daylight lasted eighteen hours, we had plenty of time to explore our forested world. We would build the greatest tree forts, float the best huckleberry rafts, and as we got older stay up all night watching the dark sky with its deep starlight splendor, complete with a bonfire and young love.

As a young boy in that magical environment, we had adventures unlimited, and since my parents enriched our lives by reading us books like *Moby Dick*, *Huckleberry Finn*, and *The Wizard of Oz*, we also had an abundance of imagination. We had imaginations that would take us to the farthest reaches of the galaxies or have us fighting the enemy of our country in a new land. No matter what we were doing, my life seemed uncomplicated, carefree, and with no responsibilities. I had no other responsibilities than those of a young boy who was bound by family protocol. I was always late for dinner since I was off on another adventure that only I could imagine. But I could not imagine what the Lord was going to bring into my life. No, I would never have imagined.

1960s

Chapter Two

A New Time, a New View

Peace comes from within. It is not a feeling but a confidence, a knowledge that no matter what happens in your life, things will be OK, and no one can take it from you. Only God can give this peace. You may give it away, you may choose to toss it aside, or you may determine to abandon that confidence. To lose your peace means that you yourself, of your own free will, or of your own wanton foolishness, misplace, set aside, or disavow that internal knowledge that was once yours. That knowledge must be "lost" by you. The Lord gives this peace to whoever asks. Ah, but you must ask. And in order to ask, you must be brought to the place of asking.

My first years were a wonderland of new life. The first October, my first autumn in the *new world*, was the most exciting time of my life. Seven years old, in my memory never having been out of the dessert landscape of Southern California, and now I was living in a land filled with colors, cooling air, rain, less sunshine, frost, more rain, clear dark nights, stars and stars, and more rain. It was exhilarating, and I was going to take it all in. My adventurous and independent spirit was released from its cage and now intended to fly and explore all that this wonderful God-created land had to offer. But first, there was school, and of course, I would now be the "new kid." Who would I meet? What would they think of me? What would I think of the kids in this *new world*? What kind of friends would I make, and of course, what would my teacher and classroom be like? Exciting thoughts, many fears, and trepidation.

I can picture when the Lord called Abraham to go to a place "He would show him," that he would be hesitant and yet at the same time excited to set out on this unknown journey. Perhaps that is why he took so long to depart and remained in the land until his father died. If we consider our feelings and fears in life, and these great men of the scriptures were men with like passions and human traits as we, then perhaps we may better understand how God deals with us. In fact, many times the Lord moves us and gives us *new worlds* to enter just like the Jews under Moses. They were given the opportunity to enter a *new world*. They did not receive the change with an open and teachable heart, and as they were given challenge after challenge, it was clear that they were many times lacking in trust and faith in what God would ultimately do for them. It is how *we* trust and receive this instruction that will dictate whether we gain wisdom, grow spiritually, and edify God, and which will ultimately give us a great blessing. The Jews were slow to learn these lessons and therefore paid some great prices. They wandered for forty years, did not receive all the lands that God had promised, and their enemies remain to this day. Obedience to the Word of God is important to our spiritual growth, and I am now sure this obedience begins from the day we are brought into this world. I grew confident with every new challenge. Perhaps, too *self*-confident.

School would be starting again soon. The summer sky was giving way to the gray clouds and drizzle that I would come to expect and love. Expect, because this was a land of rain and rainforests and love because this weather brought such wonderful results. And I for one looked forward to the snows of winter. This time of late summer was always one of great expectation. "What new classmates would I get to know and who would the new kids be?" It was always the same. I was and still am today excited to meet new people. Only today, my reasons are different. I was the new kid once, and there was nothing more exciting to me than meeting new people. What were they like? How pretty were the girls, or what new friends would follow me? Wow, school was going to start, and I would be a fourth grader.

Two years had passed since we came to this wonderful land and this most scenic city on an island. I had made many friends, especially those of my Japanese families. We were all so close that each family raised each other's children, and we learned the customs, traditions, and religions of each other. As well, we learned to respect those customs and religions and were never fearful to participate in them. My parents always encouraged us to read the Bible and research or debate the tenants of other faiths, with our "Christian" Catholic / Lutheran faith being the thermometer used to test the product of our discussions. This openness to discover our God was the foundation that the Lord used to touch me. I was so blessed to have parents who knew Christ and were not afraid to allow Him to reveal himself to us through His Word. We all got our own copies of the King James Bible and were encouraged to read and study. This was very uncommon for "Catholics."

Over the past years since my arrival, I learned to ice-skate and sled down hills that would be accomplished by either a fool or a hero. Since I never considered myself to be a fool, I must have been a hero and a most courageous one at that. My confidence grew, and my physical prowess became evident as I was able to swing a double-bladed axe, cutting down full-size Sitka spruce and "bucking" them with masterful ease. I was given a 308 British bolt-action rifle, and although I had to strip the wooden stock from the barrel to make it easier to carry, I could pack it into the forest with the best of the adults. Yes, at only nine years old, my Danish genes gave me the physical stamina and attributes any mountain man would envy, and I developed the ego to go with it. There was none greater than I and my size, and independence at that age made me a natural leader. And lead I would. With force of will if necessary, and I began to measure others by my standards. Even at nine, I forged a selfish attitude about how "I" saw people and their actions. I was the law, and what I believed is what counted. But under all that bravado and self and independence, I knew God, and as I grew, the shadow of the knowledge of who He is began to cover me.

As a "Good Catholic," I became an altar boy. I enjoyed the attention I got by being the one who helped the priest, was allowed in the alter area, and "ring the bell." I was there to serve my religion and my ego. I was, however, Byzantine, not a Roman, and my father made sure the nuns and priest knew that, as we followed a separate, more ancient ritual. We blessed from right to left, not left to right. We were baptized and confirmed after birth and by an archbishop, not the "lowly priest." I considered myself better and special. I served the ritual and not God. I still did not know, nor did I have any desire to know the Living God. I had no relationship since the religion did not teach us this. Only serve by ritual and rules. You must learn to do as the church says, not what Jesus taught.

It is important that this background is established. We all have our own backgrounds. We have those choices that we make in life based on our familial upbringing and individual "bent." We all have a particular personality, and that personality, uncontrolled by the hand of God, will manifest itself in ways yet to be seen and determined. We need guidance. If we do not get that guidance from our parents and we do not have guidance of the Holy Spirit or listen to that still small voice of the Spirit, then we will go in the direction that is our nature. And our nature is as a sinner.

This flesh will tug us in the direction that is sin and fleshly. "All we like sheep have gone astray; we have turned everyone to his own way" (Isaiah 53:6). But the verse continues with a quote of the sacrifice of Christ in the future, for our sins: "and the Lord hath laid on him the iniquity of us all." He paid the price for our iniquities. And we read in Romans, "As it is written, there is none righteous, no not one: there is none that understandeth, there is none that seeketh after God. They are all gone out of the way, they are together become unprofitable; there is none that doeth good, no, not one" (Romans 3:10–12). We cannot escape the truth of the Word of God. We can only accept the truth. "For all have sinned, and come short of the glory of God" (Romans 3: 23) For the Lord speaking through Jeremiah stated, "The heart is deceitful above all things, and desperately wicked: who can know it" (Jeremiah 17:9). God does!

I once listened to a particular Chuck Swindoll study, and he did a wonderful job, as always, of describing the nature of man and how we as children each possess and display a particular "bent" or personality profile. Some children when they are born are naturally compliant, loving, and compassionate while others may be argumentative, defiant, or independent. We each have a "bent" toward a particular personality. "Train up a child in the way he should go: and when he is old, will not depart from it" (Proverbs 22:6). So parents, "…provoke not your children to wrath: but bring them up in the nurture and admonition of the Lord" (Ephesians 6:4). We all have the capacity to do "good" by the inspiration of the Holy Spirit, but uncontrolled, we are inherently sinful. We need to be taught, raised up, and only God truly knows us, knows our "bents." Only He can truly "teach" us the way we should go, and He will do that, but He will treat us each as vastly different and separate people because we are!

The elementary school was an all-indoor school. Having spent many years in California since leaving Sitka, I had to remind myself that not all schools are outdoor designs. The weather in Sitka, one hundred inches of rain per year and snow from November to March, made it a mandate that all schools were indoors. However, we were not indoor people. During recess and lunch, we were always outside, in rain, snow, or sunshine.

The school was simple, U-shaped with the cafeteria and multipurpose room with a stage at one end of the U. The whole town used the school for small theater productions, school board meetings, town meetings, dime-a-dip dinners, evangelistic movie nights, and the like. It was truly the heart of the town, and in a small town of only two-thousand people, everybody knew everybody. The length of the school building interior had one long hallway, and each classroom was for each grade level. Classroom 1 for example was kindergarten up to room 5 for fifth grade. Sixth grade was in a separate building next to the gymnasium. It was the transition to junior high school where we learned to work with different classes and teachers. The start of our independence, so to speak. Each teacher, first through fifth, was known as that grade level teacher. If you went to second grade, you were in Mrs. Gavin's class. I was in Mrs. Gavin's when I arrived at age seven.

On the inside of the U shape of the elementary building was where the swing sets and playground equipment were located, and at the one end was the large open play field with an enclosed tennis court that was also used as a soccer court and ice-skating rink in the winter. The large open play field was dirt, or mud when it was raining (which was most of the time), and ball fields were located out away from the elementary school building. Across the street from the building was a supermarket, and yes, we had automatic doors. There were sidewalks along the road outside of the school, and next to the supermarket was the old two-story junior high school building that was at one time the high school building. Altogether a compact area chock-full of social environments with lots of activities and people. An area of town where nothing could take place that would not be noticed by many people to be reported to all by any variety of town criers.

So here I was now two years in my new home and in fourth grade. If I was independent before, now I was absolutely the most "Hey, I can do this myself, don't need nobody, and I know it all." However, what I did not know at my very mature age of nine was that I was being steadily influenced by my "friends," and that peer influence was greater than the "still small voice" of God.

Now, nine years of age may not seem like much to some, but as you may reflect, we make many critical choices in our lives that influence who we may become someday. Our childhood is critical, and the inputs we get from those we consider important are critical in shaping our spiritual lives. If it is not Christ, then it is the world.

Many times, in Samuel, Kings, and Chronicles, the Word of God gave us insights into the type of person an individual would become. Samuel was influenced by his godly mother, Solomon was influenced by his wives, and Solomon's son Rehoboam was influenced by his friends. We all have influences, and the Bible is full of examples of who made an impact in a person's life whether for God's sake or for sins. This fundamental idea is important for us to remember. For there are always those who would influence people for good or for evil? And I was certainly no exception. Like Rehoboam and many young people, we many times listen to the council of those young men and women we grew up with.

Sitka was a small town nestled on the banks of a beautiful harbor with tall mountains at its back framing in a very picturesque story book environment. As kids, we hung out many times at the docks and cold storage. This was located in the older "Indian Village" part of town. The Tlingit Indians made up a large population of this fishing village section of town. There were incredibly old homes and extremely poor fishermen from the local native population. We would watch the fishing boats unload those legendary monster halibut catches, fish off the pier, catching crab, rock cod, ling cods, and when the haring were running through the channels, the activity was fever-pitched casting and snagging two or three of the flat silver bait fish at a time, filling our buckets to the brim. These were used later for salmon and halibut fishing. So there we were, free, independent, driven by the desires of our hearts, and accountable only to our fellow adventurers. We could do anything we wished, and our self-centered, self-serving natures took the driver's seat.

The drizzly days were here as I settled into my new class. We would come to school wet and dripping and hang our coats in the closet, inside those rows of doors on one wall of the room. A real chance to get close to that person that you wanted to know. That special someone who tickled the pit of your stomach with just a look. On the other hand, you would fear the times that that person you wanted to avoid would hang their coat and place their lunch box next to yours. That meant you may have to touch them, or Lord forbid, speak to them. Or they may speak to you.

The cooler days of fall were again in the air, and all the new faces and old friends filled our classroom with that buzz of excitement. Each of us was seated at our new desks that were to be our homes and neighbors for this next year. We were getting older now, and I would be ten in a few months. And of course, even more arrogant, and even more intent on judging others by my standards or the standards established by my peers. But God had another idea. This was to be a vastly different year, and I was to begin my new lessons that only the classroom of God can teach.

Cold Storage & Indian Village

Chapter Three

Through My Eyes

Our lives are viewed through the eyes of our experiences and personal beliefs cast by the shutter over the lens of ourselves, others, or God. We see the way we are taught, are influenced, or believe. And sometimes those beliefs are self-imposed, creating the potential foundations for who we will be, whether for the good of God or bad of man. We may look at life through the eyes of others, ours, or those of God. But whose eyes we use will reveal a vastly different view.

Drizzle, drizzle, and more drizzle. Cloudy skies, wet heads, and occasional clear, cloudless beauty was slowly making way to shorter days and cooler nights. This time of year always brings a sense of change and newness for me, much like spring will do for others. I always had this deep feeling that old things must first pass away before new things can come to the forefront.

When you look at Swan Lake as the summer months dawdle by, there are very large mosquitoes buzzing and kingfishers, those small blue birds with the very large voice, diving for those small fish along the shores of an otherwise quiet and sedentary body of water. You can see the entire shoreline out to about twenty yards, covered in a rich, dark-green carpet of lily pads, their cover so dense that you do not see any water. Dragonflies skipping about dipping their tails into the wet stretches between the pads were the only clue that there was water under those large leaves floating on the surface.

And as the summer sun glowered over this small inland body of water and green trim, you can see the wear and damage of the heat and insects taking their toll on those giant flat pads. They no longer glow with lush health, but you can detect a dull display of potential death that only signals the inevitable. They will brown, rot, and slip into the depth of the deep lake, dying for the year. And you anticipate the newness that spring will bring. But first, they must die before they can become new.

As my growth into adulthood progressed, I began to view my life with a different set of eyes. Eyes that saw life as I wanted or was taught, either by friends, siblings, parents, teachers, and so on but did not yet discern the view guided by the Holy Spirit. I did not yet know God as a person and therefore did not have a relationship with Him. And as a course of fact was not open to see with His eyes, the world around me.

Now class was going to be different this year. We were learning to be more social, more interactive with the sexes. We were becoming more boys and girls, and as such, the teacher began using the ever-popular Friday square dance. This was for several reasons as I reflect, not the least, was to teach us how to follow directions. But more that we were to acknowledge the male and female roles and learn to be courteous, respectful, and gentlemanly to our counterparts. This was easy enough to do when you may have had a crush on that "beautiful red-haired girl," but what of the person or persons who did not live up to our personal expectations? Or what if someone did not particularly care to engage in this ritual with me, how was I to handle rejection? These were new ideas, and I am sure now the whole exercise was required to help us learn to deal with all aspects of social behavior. I for one had my own ideas. God had His.

All the desks get pushed aside until the entire center of the class was an open dance floor. There was plenty of room since all our classes were small in size in comparison to today's elementary classes. Open floor and all students were no longer in the privacy of their own desk and the surrounding buffer of chosen friends. You were now on display and open for all to see, to scrutinize, to examine with all your defects as you may perceive them, and they were revealed to the other children. For those with a strong self-confidence, much like an alpha male in a pack animal environment, it was an opportunity to exert his dominance, but for the most of use with maturing ideals about who we are or how we are to act, it was downright intimidating.

We still do this today, and many times we continue to handle these social discomforts in much the same way as we learned to do as children. However we had coped then, we continue to do the same things only as grown-ups, that is to say, we do not act like children…or do we? I have been reading a book by Milan and Kay Yerkovich called *How We Love*. It is a book that shares how our early childhood and familial experiences shape and influence, or maybe better said, impact, how we respond to our lives and others, throughout our adult lives…unless the Holy Spirit takes control and changes our eyesight and heart. Here we were, to dance with a partner, but this being square dancing, we would exchange and redirect partners, allowing us to become partners to many girls whether we wanted to or not, and at times have physical contact with them. What an invasion of my personal choices. Besides, there were always one or two girls, or for that matter, boys, whom you may not want to be that close to. Oh Lord, help me not to have to touch that one person that I find objectionable for my own reasons.

Our peers have a great influence on how we see and perceive life around us. Desiring to please others, our friends, and belong to a group is a strong magnet by which we see our life around us. Others influence us to take actions or inaction based on our acceptance. And at this time in my life, I was not so in tune with the Spirit available to me and the need to please Him and the acceptance of His nature and that agape love He can give us through that relationship with the Lord. Therefore, we move through life and grow in the knowledge of interactions and relationships as seen through our personal social glasses unless something changes. Or I gain new insights by the use of a new set of eyewear—or better, heart-wear.

So there you have it. Forced to "act" like you may enjoy the company of another when in fact you have no desire to look upon much less touch certain persons. Why do we do this? Why do we look at our fellow men as if they are a disease that can be caught? Why do we make such judgments without reason, and why do we look out through such eyes? Eyes that deceive us and cast only shadows on our ability to see, only what our hearts may interpret, unless we change the aperture of our heart and take in a greater depth of field.

As a reminder, the Lord tells us, "The heart is deceitful above all things, and desperately wicked: who can know it" (Jeremiah 17:9). That is why we cannot discern the truth. But God looks upon the heart and not on the outside. He sees what can be. He sees what He will sculpt into a masterpiece. The potter with a lump of clay. We, on the other hand, only look on the outward man. And even if we were to try, our wicked heart has a self-adjusting lens. A lens adjusted by our interpretation of any situation. We see through our eyes. We adjust that lens through our reduced lighting distorted focus.

I am so thankful that God's eyes look on our hearts and not on what we are, because we fail Him over and over. He looks on us as the finished work He will perform. He looks on a weak, sinful creation, a lump of clay for the Master Potter's hands, a blank canvas that a beautiful painting can be created, a piece of rock to be sculpted into a work of art, a piece of impure silver or gold that will need to be heated to remove the dross and imperfections until perfected. The Word of God refers to this over and over. "But now, O Lord, thou art our father; we are the clay, and thou our potter; and we all are the work of thy hand" (Isaiah 64:8). "Hath not the potter power over the clay, of the same lump to make one vessel unto honor, and another unto dishonor?" (Romans 9:21). "Shall the clay say to him that fashioneth it, What makest thou?" (Isaiah 45:9). "And I will bring the third part through the fire, and will try them as silver is refined, and will try them as gold is tried" (Zechariah 13:9). "And I will turn my hand upon tee, and 'thoroughly' purge away thy dross, and take away all thy tin" (Isaiah 1:25).

So, as I continue to share my story, perhaps you will begin to focus on how the Lord leads, guides, and refines us to see through his eyes. How his refining and pottery work will put our lives in his handiwork to create in us His workmanship, in Christ Jesus our Lord. Sometimes it is the spinning of the potter's wheel and the gentle work of the Lord's hands, but sometimes the temperature of the furnace needs to increase to remove the dross of sin and refine us to be more like Him. I pray the remainder of this story will give you clearer, cleaner lenses.

During recess, Friday dance day, peer groups, and simple childhood interactions, I was learning to discern beauty and truth by the outward person. Not on the inward heart as the Lord does. And as a course of consequence, I, too, was rejecting of an Alaskan Indian girl (I believe she was of Thlinket Indian heritage) by the name of Verna Lewis. Even her name sounded ugly to me. Everybody treated her as if she were the ugliest person on this earth. Oh, how cruel we were, but it seemed ever so natural to my understanding. Because she was from the Indian tribes of the city, she also lived on the waterfront area by the docks known as Indian Village. Much like our south 48, this was akin to their reservation and was poor, living in not-so-sound housing structures, actually some considered unsafe. And the smell of fish, since most of the people here were fishermen and hunters by tradition.

Verna was a "plain Jane" and wore those long, below-the-knee, one-piece flower dresses of the typical cotton fabric that denoted either they were secondhand, thrift shop dresses, or hand-made by her family. Her hair was jet black, oily, and hung straight with bangs, and at nine or ten years old, she was gangly and awkward looking. The kids use to call her Zombie. They would chant, "Here comes Zombie." They would even follow her around calling her that name. How sad as I remember vividly, the pain it must have caused her. Now I did not know what the word *zombie* meant, but I would chime in, just like the rest. I think back to how I treated her. Today, my heart breaks that I participated in such cruel behavior. Her memory of those times, to this day, brings tears to my eyes. I am so glad God does not treat us that way. He died for *all* of us. And through His eyes, she was His beautiful child. But through my eyes, she was detestable, ugly, and someone to avoid.

She was by my standards ugly and someone to avoid. And I hung around with some pretty ugly kids. Remember, I was it! So when Friday came, I did everything I could to avoid even being near her, much less touching her during our Friday ritual of dance and social interaction. I did not look forward to the square-dancing time. I might have to be her partner. But our loving Lord had other ideas for me. Remember the refining process. Well, He was to soon knock some sense into me.

31

Chapter Four

Changing Eyesight

There is no change without pain. If we are comfortable, we tend to stay in a comfortable place. We do not like what hurts, and yet without painful events, we will not move to a better place. Change is good, only if it moves us closer to God, and God knows how to strategically use the ox-goad.

Such a small island city of two thousand to three thousand residents. Only a few small churches and the Catholic church, only a few hundred yards down the street, toward the harbor, from the junior high school, was the religious haven of the city's complement of Roman Catholics, with the exception of our family. Oh yes, we were Catholics, but of course Byzantine, not Roman. This was to become a small enlightenment at a later time. And I became a dedicated altar boy. Arriving early to help dress the priest and of course get into my vestments. I was going to "serve" my religion…and God. These memories still loom large in my memory and help grind the spiritual lenses of my eyesight. But not in a manner that I was to suspect.

"No Sunday paper and comics until *after* church," came the words, harsh and firm, but loving from my father. And off we all went to that little Roman Catholic Church. It probably only held a maximum of fifty people. The front porch was an A-shaped roof, and the eve hung over the entrance, maybe a few feet long. If it were raining or snowing, a large family like ours would not all fit to protect us from the elements, if the door were not yet open. There was the priest and a couple of nuns. So they did not always open the doors early. When the priest or nun opened the door, we all skittered into the church and most often took up temporary residence in the first couple of pews, as was my father's custom. If I were to serve that day, I would have already been headed to the back rooms to fulfill my responsibilities and prepare the altar. Mass was at 6:30 a.m., later like 10:00 a.m. and an evening 6:00 p.m. mass. The early and evening masses were not heavily attended. In fact, there were times that the 6:30 a.m. mass might not even have any attendees, especially in rainy or cold, snowy weather, but the priest still preside over the mass. It was usually too early for any altar boy to assist so he did everything himself. He was dedicated to serve the church ritual. And never missed a day, seven days a week.

Now, at this time in my life and because my father and mother put a desire to know God in our lives, I genuinely wanted to know who the Lord was. Perhaps He himself put that desire into my heart, but nonetheless,

I wanted to understand the one who created our world, universe, and selves. I know at these younger years, it was not something all young people were thinking a lot about, but I found myself asking, a lot, who I was and how I can serve this Great God my folks put so much faith in. Do not ever underestimate the power of parental influence. And yet, the tug of this world was to be a continuing distraction from my potential relationship with the Creator of the Universe. I often wondered if we were brought to Alaska and this small, picturesque city so I might learn of Him. "Take my yoke upon you, and learn of me; for I am meek and lowly in heart" (Matthew 11:29). By sharing these times, I would grow closer in faith to better serve Him later in my life. Jesus teaches us through life lessons. His parables show us our relationship to Him on a human level. A level we would be able to more readily understand. So I found myself asking about Him and spending many days and nights alone with a deep desire to commune with God. This becomes so important, as I reflect on this part of my life and perhaps others can reflect on times and seasons that drew themselves closer to a relationship with a True and Living God.

As the years were to roll on before I was yet ten years old, I found several places of quiet rest and contemplation. I always had a strong desire to learn of the Lord's creation because I felt that His creation yields who He is. The designer, builder, and ever long-suffering and merciful creator of our universe. He established rules, orders, and laws for the world and life we were to live. So I found a small bluff or saddle-like outcropping that overhung the lake on a high hill area. I had a wonderful view of the lake and shoreline, the sky at day and night with berry bushes around me to enjoy those wonderful summer fruits of blueberries, salmonberries, and huckleberries to feed my body while I was praying for God to reach and feed my soul. He was going to work on how I see things, as I think back now.

I would come to my space many times. I would watch the kingfisher catch small fish in the lake, fish jumping, dragonflies darting about, and being bit by the largest mosquitoes in the world. But these bloodsucking pests would not deter me from my mission. In the summer, it was quiet and peacefully warm. Lazy days of just idle contemplation. The grass on the knoll was cozy and not wet for once, since in the summer months, it did not rain, and the temperatures were quite warm. At least to a lad who was used to subzero and wet weather. This was a nice change for sure, but it also allowed me many long daylight hours to consider my thoughts and the creation around me.

Why do I continue to digress like this? I have a lot to share. Because as I spent the seasons on my perch, observing all that the Lord created, I began to see things differently. I began to look at what He created through a different set of lenses, to begin to see as He would show me. And I greatly enjoyed His insights, I believe given to me for a future purpose.

Sitting here on my small saddle-type outcropping of grass, under and surrounded by berry bushes, I watch an eagle in a tree. Beautiful and majestic as it perches. Wings tucked aside its body. Eyes sharp and its head looking to and fro, rotating almost 360 degrees, observing the surroundings and especially the water of Swan Lake below. This large powerful-looking bird surveying the world within its sight. Much like we do, I am doing, on the side of this hill. Looking, sitting still, observing the world around us with the gifts, the eyes, and senses the Lord has given us. Sitting, watching…but then, something so magnificent and magical happens.

This beautiful creation sitting there like a statue, stoic and majestic, drops off the limb, and the seven-plus foot wingspan opens to full view, and the eagle soars to catch a fish from the waters of the lake below. We see the potential and beauty that was kept hidden by the wings tucked alongside the body. If that bird had not spread its wings and used the design, the gift of flight that God had given it, we would not have seen the full potential of this beautiful creation. Many times, we live our lives with the gifts God gave us tucked away. Only when we trust the Lord, spread our "wings," and fly with the gifts God gave us can we truly "see" our other potentials.

When an eagle chick hatches, it's totally dependent upon the love and care of the parent. As it grows and the downy fluff of developing feathers turns to defined eagle feathers, and the young eaglet grows stronger, it begins to spread those still developing designs of flight that will later carry it for hundreds of miles across the sky. But before that happens, the young growing bird must learn to fly, on its own, and become independent, confident, and dependent upon the gifts it has been given.

The nest hangs on the ledge of a cliff, hundreds of feet up or on the top of a great tree almost one hundred and fifty feet above the ground, having been incubated through the cold of winter, hatched in early, but a very cold spring, and observes the dedicated, long-suffering process of protection and parenting. But as safe as it feels, the young soon-to-be majestic bird, with talons the size of a man's hands, must learn to fly. At first sight, the eagle nest location appears to be one of safekeeping from predators, but on deeper consideration, what better place must this bird start out to accomplish its mastery of the gifts that were given than a place that will give the young eagle a manner for which to learn how to fly and spread its wings. When it is time, the parent aids the young eagle out of the nest to begin the long drop to potential death. It must learn to spread and use those magnificent wings and sore far above its nest, its only known home. The wonderful thing to watch is how, at the very final moment, if the youngster has not yet learned to trust its newfound purpose, the parent eagle swoops down to pick it out of the sky with those large, hand-size talons and take it back up to the nest. Where the lesson continues anew until that young eagle finally, finally stretches those magnificent wings with success and soars on its own. Some learn quickly, some take more time, but they will all sooner or later learn or…

As my eyes would take in this process of teaching the young eagle to fly, it seems from my viewpoint to be an extremely dangerous and fear-filled testing to success. The young bird has no understanding what is at first taking place and must see the ground coming up fast thinking, "Is my father trying to kill me, scare me, treat me so cruelly?" Some nestlings learn to spread their wings and trust the parent in very few tries, but some take many "drops" or "falls" to grasp the lesson, but the nestling learns to trust. The father never allows the young eagle to be harmed by the ground no matter how close it gets; he never gives him more than he can handle but with the test, gives him a way out…spread those wings and fly, learn and trust the parent to protect and always catch him before he hits the ground.

*****

It is another day, another Friday, and another square dance. Kids can be cruel. I can see that now. But back then, I had much to learn. As I reflect on my past learning today, I can now see what the Lord was doing for me—answering my prayers. We do not know what the future will hold for us or how we can travel this gift of life. A master chess player can look at potential moves on the chess board and see the next move to take. He can see the consequences of many moves in advance and knows the outcomes. I have had many discussions with folks who cannot understand how God can give us free will, the freedom to make our own choices, and live with those consequences while answering our prayers. And as a teacher, I used to share with my young high school students how they do not have to endure the consequences of poor or bad choices because we, their fathers, friends, grandparents, teachers, and godly leaders traveled those roads already and can now share the fallacy of trying to find out for yourself what will happen from an unguided decision. The Lord is the master chess player, and He knows the results of every possible move we can and will eventually make. We have the choice to make them, but when you ask Him for help, the game of life can be much more successful, or it can be a long, grinding chess game of making the wrong moves.

Now when I began to be aware that God is indeed with us, and I wanted to serve Him, I was yet a young boy. I feel we all are given an awareness of God. We are designed to want to know him, but just as Christ, the living word was sent to dwell among us, to teach us, and to serve as a sacrifice for our sins, getting to know Jesus must be taught to us. "For as the rain cometh down, and the snow from heaven, and returneth not thither, but watereth the earth, and maketh it bring forth and bud, that it may give seed to the sower, and bread to the eater: So shall my word be that goeth forth out of mouth: it shall not return unto me void, but it shall accomplish that which I please, and it shall prosper in the thing whereto I sent it" (Isaiah 55:10–11 NKJV). So it is that we must be shown the gospel so we may accept Him and His Spirit to dwell within us. Nevertheless, the Lord does hear us cry out to him and does answer our needs. And so it was with me. I shared my Catholic traditions because, for all the good the church's customs and traditions were, it was still lacking in how to teach its flock how to really know God. I wanted to really know who God was but did not know where to start. My culture, my church, my parents did not know how to teach me what I wanted to learn, so I asked God to show me and teach me. I wanted to really know and understand who our creator was.

On one of those square dance Fridays, we were all once again engaged in dancing with other partners, and once again I found myself face-to-face with Verna Lewis. And as always, I reflected on the outward appearance of this girl with disdain. Boy was I in for a teaching moment surprise at lunch. God was about to answer my prayer of learning who He is and how He sees us.

Family Christmas 1963

Chapter Five

A Powerful Teaching Moment

There are moments in time that we sometimes call teachable moments. And sometimes those moments can be very painful, but most memorable. And most teachable.

Rain, rain, and more rain. In a place that gets one hundred inches of rain a year, you get used to what we call liquid sunshine. But today, this particular day, the rain would remind me throughout my life, of much, much more. This day of drizzle would be so different and most memorable for me. This day would be as if the Lord were drenching me with tears for both what I would do and what He had to allow. And I would never forget the lesson He was to teach me. This drizzle, tear-filled day was to be the answer to my prayers and the beginning of my long road to really getting to know God.

Another square-dancing Friday. Move the desks, line up, and…there was Verna. Across from me. Verna Lewis. Zombie! How unlucky could I get. This would not be good for me. I would have to show the kids that I was not going to be forced to like her. Or even touch her. So when lunchtime came, I got involved with the other kids, cruel kids, and followed her around the playground, on the street by the market, and anywhere we would see her and shouting, "Zombie, Zombie!" Even today, my heart sinks and hurts to think I really engaged in that behavior. How could I go along with such mean and cruel activities? But I did. Of course, I really did not know what the word *zombie* meant, but I was going to call her that anyway because the other boys were calling her that. And I did not think twice to notice the hurt and pain on her face and those who were her girlfriends. I had poor eyesight indeed.

As is typical of lunch recess, there was a teacher monitoring the activities of the students. On this particular day, the teacher was a sixth-grade teacher from classrooms at the far end of the playground. She was not familiar with the younger students, and I am quite sure she ran a tight ship of a classroom environment. She was one of those teachers who did not tolerate the kind of behavior I was exhibiting toward this Native American girl. And the Lord was going to use her to really teach me a lesson—an exceptionally painful lesson I would never forget.

I do not know who she was, her name, or anything about her as a teacher, but she grabbed me when I was yelling at Verna near the school building. She and a friend were walking on the sidewalk, together across the street by the market. It was drizzling, a typical drizzly, gray day. The teacher had an umbrella. My friend Mark was nearby, so he witnessed the whole event. And since he was one of my close friends, and his mother had been my second-grade teacher, the repercussions would be pretty lasting for both me and the teacher. She got incredibly angry and quickly told me about my abhorrent behavior, never releasing me from her grip and commencing to slap my mouth over and over until it was bloody. Now remember, this was in the sixties, and today I do not know if that was considered normal behavior for any teacher, but I sure knew this was not the kind of action even my father would do. And trust me, he was not afraid to punish us. He would use his wide belt as a strap, but only when we deserved it and never in anger. He would wait until his anger subsided and then shared why we got the punishment. It was a learning experience. There is no change without pain. God makes that biblically clear.

Maybe my actions struck a painful chord, or maybe she felt this was an appropriate way to teach me not to be so cruel, I do not know. And I do not remember exactly why or when she stopped, but she kept slapping my mouth over and over, and my head was whipping side to side, and I could taste blood. She muttered something about calling anyone names. And in particular, that name. I don't know whether my friend Mark, who was very tall for his age, because his parents were very tall, stepped in, said something, or she just stopped on her own, but suddenly, as quickly as she began, she stopped and released me. For a short moment, that seemed to last forever, I remember just looking into her eyes. I do not remember if I just ran or I walked away or what happened next. It was all a blur, and the rest of the day was a blur. I do not even know if I went back to class or just left school, but I could feel my mouth swelling and tasting the blood. It hurt, but my pride, my prideful heart, was hurt even more.

Our family usually had dinner together at our wooden picnic table in the dining area of the large living area. So everyone who sat at dinner was on display for view and discussion. Again, it was the same on this evening, and I was not eager to come to dinner, but my father's whistle summoned us all to "home base." As a large family of six kids, well five who were always out and about, since Jonathan was still too small to go out and about. Timothy was pretty young, but we were all pretty independent, and he could be anywhere near home. I remember my father putting his finger between his teeth and blowing a most loud screeching whistle in a very specific rhythmic pattern. We all knew that whistle when we heard it, and it traveled very far. We would all stop what we were doing, looking like meerkats on the African planes. Listening intently and without hesitation would drop what we were doing, tell the other kids we have to go, Dad is calling, and off we would head home. As adults today, we still talk of that time and that whistle. Today, this behavior reminds me of Jesus's words, "My sheep hear my voice, and I know them, and they follow me" (John 10:27).

So there I sat at the dinner table, mouth obviously very swollen, a split lip where earlier blood spilled out on my shirt, my head hung down and tears in my eyes from embarrassment. None of this escaped the gaze of my father and the rest of the family. Of course, my father thought immediately, with my wild past behavior, I had gotten into a fight with one of the kids at school. This of course was the direction his initial inquiry was headed with those stern eyes cast at me. "I hope the other guy looks worse than you do," was his first words. I started crying with shame and quietly said that I did not get in a fight.

I began to explain what had transpired at school and why I looked like this. He became furious! He said, "What you did was so wrong, but even I would not draw blood from my son in reprimand or punishment. I am going to see the school about this." And that was the last I heard of the issue except for talk from students that the teacher was fired. I really felt bad for her because I, at that point and much more time for the Lord to work on my conscience, understood her anger. Because of me, I caused her life greater sadness. I didn't understand my feelings because before this I would have never given it a second thought and figured, "She got what was coming," but now I felt shame and sadness. Why?

*****

On the main highway, Halibut Point Road, at the feet of our horseshoe-shaped tract homes was a large lot where the Baptist church was located. It was set back, and the large lawn was along the main highway. On one side of the property was a street that went from the high-way to the top of a small hill. I don't remember what the street name was because us kids only called it Bunker Hill because at the top was Annie Bunker's house. In the winter, it was so slippery with the snow and ice pack that no cars except with large chains could even get halfway up. Needless to say, this was the perfect sledding hill. And we would station kids at the base of the hill to watch for traffic. As we came down the hill at a very high rate of speed, we would either get a wave to keep going, jump off the other end of the street into the snowy meadow on the other side, and crash to a stop. But if traffic was coming, we would be waved off, and the Baptist church lawn area was the perfect rollover safety stop.

I always see metaphors for much of God's hand in my life. Events, seasons, things, places that tell a story or make one consider what this means in the world. Looking back, this annual event of crash or succeed was part of another life lesson, especially since you were "safe" when you rolled to a stop in front of God's house. God was there to protect you, no matter what road you took, but even in His presence and protection, you may still have to bear the consequence of your choices. The Holy Spirit would always be there to come alongside you and comfort you. Crashing either safely on the lawn or over the road, that soft snow was always there to comfort my crash or roll.

That Baptist church was really the center of many town activities, including Sunday schools, summer vacation Bible school, and the often-held evening Baptist Bible movie night, held at the elementary school auditorium but sponsored by the Baptist church. These were Christian movies that the pastors used to hold for prodding people to want to accept Jesus or at the least ask for prayer. It was at one of these movie nights that our family attended that I had my first real encounter with Jesus. My parents loved the Lord, and any way we got biblical teaching was good with them. I was at one of those nights after the movie, and to this day could not tell you what the movie was about. They asked the same question as usual: do you want to know God? I guess the Lord had prepared my heart with Verna and all, but I was always very sensitive to wanting to know, really know who Jesus, the Lord, was. Not just how my religion saw him but how others did. How I might be able to know him. How the Bible told me He was. How He saw us! My young heart was now ready to really, really begin a journey to open my eyes. When the pastor asked who wanted to accept Jesus (and I really did want to know how to serve Him, not just as an altar boy), I looked up at my dad and mom, and they both said, "Go ahead if your heart is leading you." Now this was not at a Catholic church; this was at a Baptist movie night. We were not Baptists. We were Byzantine Catholics with a Lutheran mother. But the thing that the Lord gave me, blessed my life for the future, were two parents who wanted their children to know the Lord, no matter who showed them the way. I suppose you could say, they truly knew that you had to raise up your children in the way "they" should go. They never put us in a mold. I thank God today for my parents! They are both gone now, but I am quite sure they are with the Lord as good and faithful servants.

That next morning, it was raining pretty good. But when I woke up, I was determined to serve the Lord the only way I knew how. So I put on my clothes and especially my boots; we all wore rubber boots and quickly left the house and walked to my Catholic church. The priest always held six o'clock morning mass, no matter who attended, and I was determined to serve mass, since the priest never had an altar boy to help that early in the morning, I felt it was the perfect opportunity to serve where there was no service. I stood on the front steps under the small roof covering, in the rain, waiting for the door to be opened. And then I darted in, out of the wet, dark weather (it seemed like it was always wet and dark), got on my robes, and did my duty. I do not remember if any word were exchanged between me and the priest, but I went about my responsibilities with the expert knowledge of a seasoned altar boy. How many days I did this or for how long, I do not remember, but that first day is burned into my memory to this day, and the delight I got from doing something for God is still a part of my heart. I am not sure, but I could not have been much more than nine years old. But that was the start of my new life in wanting to see God with different eyes. And my heart was changing from that Byzantine Catholic altar boy to someone who felt, really felt, and empathized with the pain of others. I could not explain it, but it was as if the feeling of others flowed through me and I knew how they felt. That sounds funny as I write this, but looking back, I had to forcefully set aside those feelings in order be "sinful." I promised the Lord that I never wanted to be that old kid again but to see what He wanted for me. And so another lesson session began.

PBY at the Turn Around

Chapter Six

Create in Me a New Heart Oh God

When you prepare the soil for planting, the turning of the soil is not done only once, but it must be tended and prepared throughout all seasons. Nothing new can grow unless the soil is fertilized, tended, and watered. And you must look to be shown the weeds that must be removed, lest they choke out the good crop.

Now where to start: how to find a right way to know how God wants me to be. I only know how my Catholic traditions gave me "religiosity" as I call it today. Then it was simply my faith or culture. Most folks in religious life have Bibles. I only had one of those New Testament, small Bibles that you get from. Well, I did not really know where you get it from, I was just given it, if I remember correctly, by my parents when I was six. But it could have come from anyone. It was all I had, next to my dad's Catholic missal or the mass books in the church. I accepted the desire to know God outside of my religion, as my religion was mainly customs and culture, rules, and what to "do" to gain God's favor, but I really did not know how or who was going to teach me. The priest only seemed to understand being a Catholic and how to do mass. Any time I heard him discuss the Bible or God, it was in the context of what the Catholic church says to do, such as to earn favor or some rule as in baptism or confirmation, and even then, the Romans and the Greeks didn't seem to agree on that. Bless left to right or right to left. I really felt that I had a dilemma. How do I get to know God? And I really wanted to know Him!

So first answered prayer. Maybe because my parents were there when I prayed at that movie night, or maybe because it was a "tradition" of my mom's Lutheran faith, or maybe it was just the Lord touching my parents' heart, but whatever the reason, it was answered prayer. My parents presented me with my own King James leather zip-up Bible with my name embossed on the outside cover. And I began to read the pages from page 1, chapter 1 of Geneses to try and learn. To take of Him and learn of Him!

******

Now it was another Friday square dance day. Push the desks back and get ready to interact, to dance, and yes, touch Verna. But this time, for some reason, and I understand now, but not then, not really, I was going to see things a little different. When I looked at Verna Lewis; she wasn't the same girl as I looked at before. She took my hand and danced with me as if I had not said those horrible things or treated her with such disdain. She had a smile so kind and looked at me with kind eyes. I suppose I didn't yet understand forgiveness. Oh, yes, we talked about our sins being forgiven every Easter, but at that age, I did not yet understand what that meant or what forgiveness looked like. Yet when I looked into her eyes, it was as if she was sharing with me a feeling that I can only describe with today's knowledge, as agape love and forgiveness. She was sharing a gift that I was later to learn could only come from God.

Now, I did not understand how someone so young and not from my religion could know this. But whatever it was that she had, I wanted it. Because I was beginning to feel her pain and heartache and the pain I inflicted on so many kids over my few short years. I knew I had a lot to learn, and maybe this person could teach me. It was as if I was beginning to gain the opportunity to see through another set of lenses. As if my soul was being filled with the ability to feel the pain of others. It was as if she had given me a gift through her kind eyes. Her eyes looked so gentle, caring, and, I still did not understand, forgiving. At that age, I would have felt like she was not "holding a grudge." That felt nice. It felt comforting. I wanted others to feel the same thing.

We became fast friends, Verna and me. I enjoyed just being around her, square-dancing with her, and yet I have no memory of us ever having any discussions. She just made me feel accepted, even though it was me who had been the unaccepting one. When I looked into those eyes, and I could not today tell you what color they were, I just saw kindness, happiness, gentleness, and I suppose that is why she had other students who just enjoyed being around her. I know it sounds a bit, well I don't know, but I have carried those few short moments close to my heart since then. Even today, when I see someone in pain, hurt, sad, and the like, I reflect on Verna Lewis and the gift she gave me. Or at least I always believed it was from her, but as time continued to move me along life like a river, I learned that God has ways of using events, times, circumstances, and people to give us gifts from His Holy Spirit. Until this writing, I have never shared this with anyone. And later I was to understand that the Lord was answering my prayers, through Verna, the prayers that asked Him if I could just serve Him, any way, any time, any place He needed me.

*****

Yes, I was so excited. Another Friday, another square dancing, and another chance to see, to hold, and "see" Verna. I was now really looking forward to this, what I now considered our special day. Interesting that all these events happened quickly one after another. An order of event coming one right after the other. There was no delay, as if the events I was to be a part of required a particular timeline. Perhaps so I would be able to connect the lessons as in a procedure required to learn a particular lesson. Or shared events to become lasting and indelible, before the ink dries on the paper of my memory. I was excited about all that had happened to me, to help me learn to care about others, just as Verna cared about others, and her eyes reflected those lessons with deeper feelings that would never disappear, no matter how old and yellow the pages became. Tomorrow would be another day.

But no Verna. Not today. I always enjoyed dancing with her. Just seeing her. I could not explain it, but I was happy to be around her. She always seemed to be at peace and, how can I say it, joy-filled. She always was like that, but I could not see her for what she was, how she even accepted me, even when I was mean to her. She just seemed special. Oh, well, I will see her tomorrow. But I missed her today.

Tomorrow was here, yes, square dance day, but again…no Verna? No Verna, another day, and no Verna. How could that be? She had never been sick, and she never missed a day much less two. And never missed square dance day. But no Verna. And my heart was sad because in my own little boy way, I was learning from her.

That afternoon, the teacher called us all over for an announcement. She shared with us that Verna would no longer be coming to class with us. I was heartbroken. Me, sad? About a girl like Verna?

Then she continued…there had been a fire in the Indian Village, and we were told the story that I still remember to this day, and my eyes filled with tears. Lots of tears. I was not only heartbroken but angry, lost, and empty all at once. God must really not like me. And the big question…why?

Why? We often ask God that question, don't we? Why? Pastors, parents, and older wiser folks often share that we don't always know the answers to why; only God does. He knows the before, then, and after of all our lives, and he understands how these times can be used for our teaching, learning, maturity in Christ, and our growth in faith. He knows and we are to simply have faith that it will all work out. But that does not stop the whys of a child's heart. Maybe later, but not now. But plant the seed, and it will grow with the proper watering.

Sitka Down Town at St Michaels

Chapter Seven

My Loss and God's Gain

God doesn't lose anything; He gains. He created this universe, this world, us, and our futures. He is perfect and makes all things perfect in His own way and timing. Perhaps we look at things through the wrong set of eyes. Our losses may be how He creates the gains.

The story we were told that day was not what we expected. Well, not what we may have expected at that time, but on reflection, it was what I would have expected, being that God allowed me to know who Verna was or at least what I remember. I do not know to this day, whether Verna knew the Lord or was a Christian as our denominational understanding would tell us and at her age if she even was given the chance to learn about Jesus, but who she was, was a testimony of a person who must have had some understanding of the belief of God. I still believe that.

We were told that there was a fire in the village, and a home was engulfed in flames. These buildings were old and burn easily. The family that Verna was a part of was a large one with several siblings. Verna was the older child, and her quiet countenance would not only have been a revelation of her actions but the strength of her character, as I came to know her. These would frame her actions.

As the house burned, Verna realized her younger siblings were still in the house, so she, without considering the consequences of her actions, went back into the engulfed house to help her family. No one came out. All were lost, including Verna.

I am often reminded of the words of Jesus, *"Greater love hath no man than this, that a man lay down his life for his friends"* (John 15:13 KJV). In this case, it was her siblings. Her short life reflected a life of love, and her final act proved that. She endured ridicule from me and disdain from peers, but her unwavering vision for what is right, and a gentle spirit, today I can only say she saw with the Eyes of God.

I was shattered. I felt angry, lost, and so saddened. I gave my life to the Lord. I wanted to serve Him. I was an altar boy. And as the days and years meandered on, that word "I" began to be washed away from the pages of my story, of my life. This one time in my life left raw, unwritten expectations for who I would become. It was an unwashable, time-transcending mark on my life. My actions for the rest of my life were dictated by this singular point in my life. I realize this must sound melodramatic but from a boy's eyes, to a teen's eyes, to a young man's eyes, and now as a much older man, that is how I would have and do now see this precious point in time.

As life went on, I would reflect on Verna. I never shared my thoughts with anyone, but they were always there. A lesson learned and perhaps an answer to prayer after I had given the Lord my life. Now I am not saying I lived an overwhelming godly life, but the Spirit would always bring me back to that time as a reminder of my original desire to serve the Lord and to better understand what love is. You cannot see the way God does unless you can look into the heart of people, maybe even "feel' what others feel. You know, when you get a new pair of glasses, it is wonderful how clear things become.

So God did not lose anyone, and His thoughts are not our thoughts, neither His ways are our ways, and whatever He sets to accomplish is eventually for our good, even if we cannot see it. "The Lord seeth not as man seeth; for man looketh on the outward appearance, but the Lord looketh on the heart" (1 Samuel 16:7 KJV).

I spent many years considering these things. God sees things differently because He is eternal. He is in the past, now, and the future. We see death and the effects on our lives. Death is for us who live on this earth, live in this flesh, live in this life. Physical death is not the end of our existence, only the departure of this existence. Our soul lives on. If you believe in Christ, you will live with Christ. If you do not, you will live on without Him. If we here on earth do not see as the Lord sees, we live almost hopeless. To that person who has no hope, there is pain and loss. But to the Lord, your earthly death is gain, your time to live with Christ. It may seem to us a loss of that person but that person and God's gain.

And that gain can be even more for us in this world as I was to learn. Verna was a loss to me, family, friends, and others in this small community, but the lessons we learn and will continue to learn are our gains from this sacrifice. And over the years, when I ask, I want to know what love is, then this time, season episode, that the Lord choreographed, as a moment to see how the Lord sees, will many times overcome my thoughts as though the Lord brings her life to my remembrance. And then, to use the memory, He continues to sharpen the focus of my relationship so I may see through his eyes.

Sitka-Alaska-Town

Chapter Eight

Lessons Learned Gifts Given

God deals with us all individually and raises us up according to our bent/the way that we go. We all can say we have similar stories, but what do we learn? The Lord teaches us all differently and gives us gifts for His glory.

Jesus wants us all to be more like Him. He wants to have fellowship with us; He wants us to be Holy as He is Holy. The Lord, in his infinite wisdom, knows who we are and how we "work." After all, He created us, created me, but our growth is an ongoing process. Physically, we first learn to lift up our head, then we roll over, crawl, then stand up, walk, run, and as our physical bodies gain strength and coordination, we are able to do wonderful physical feats with the bodily gift He gave us. We are fearfully and wonderfully made with so much physical potential. But we had to start by lifting up our heads.

Interesting…lifting up our heads. To the Lord? Oh yes, even though we may not have recognized it yet, we start by lifting up our heads. And so we must start on our spiritual growth in the same way. Just as every child grows at different rates, so do we. Just as we all have a start to the use of those physical gifts, so will we also start our spiritual growth and not every starting line is the same for each person. We are all different, and the Lord tailors our learning. Our gifts to our personal natures for His service and His glory.

We must begin our growth by opening our eyes. Seeing with His eyes, through His eyes. Jesus was many times reminding the Jews, the apostles, and us that you need to see with your eyes, the things of God, the ways of the Lord. Don't be blind leading the blind, and look on the inward man, the heart.

It was no happenstance, no serendipity as one might say, that my father and mother moved to this small town in Alaska. From as far back as I could remember, and I can remember times as young as when I was two years old, I was so very much aware of the Lord in my life. Whether it was because of the traditions and religious customs of my father, the depth of reading the word inspired by my mother, or if as so many people say today, "God loves you and has a plan for your life," I do not know, but I knew He was there, somewhere, somehow, and I was always awed by His creation. Wanting to serve Him was a goal I have always desired, even to this day. Ah yes, I dropped a few plates and stumbled over the carpet, ever simply forgot to get up on time or just plain chose not to do the servant's job, but my heart truly wanted to serve Him. And maybe so many of us as we get to know the Lord wants to serve Him. Unfortunately, we as flawed, selfish individuals think we should be a Billy Graham or Chuck Smith or Steven Curtis Chapman. We live in a world of billions of people and Jesus would not have any loss but all to come to Him, and since He wants to use us, to allow us to serve and participate in that great work, there are many ways to serve.

What I may not have understood and many of us may still be trying to understand is what God has in store for us. And that is, that since He did have a plan for my life, He had that plan since I was born, and He was going to give me the tools to use for His service. He was going to work with my individuality. He was going to do work that would forever influence my thoughts and give me a new set of eyes. He was going to use this wonderful young girl, Verna, to create in me a new heart and eyes. Just as He might do for all who want to know His will for our lives.

Now as I share the completion of this chapter in my life I am trying to share what I learned, so maybe if there is someone who continues to wonder what God has in mind for them, they might reflect on this example and consider, just consider, the plan He has for you may be more simple but ever so important to the master plan of Jesus, that none should be lost. That He can and does use you and gives you the tools to do His work, but we may not be seeing what He sees. You and I are created for His purpose. So it is God who has the plan. Just as the Bible shares those stories, but throughout the Word of God, there were people you read that seemed to be profoundly used, like David, but David was only usable if Rehab helped the spies and was part of the Messianic line. Or that Saul's son Johnathan befriended him or he spent his early tears as a shepherd, or Abigail brought his men provisions, became his wife, and her son may have potentially influenced those in the lineage of Jesus. You see, we are all part of his plan, and as Rehab trusted God to do her part, and it was the declaration of her faith in God through the observation of the fear of Israel, she by faith trusted the Lord's use for her. I learned that we all have periods, points in time, season, or circumstances where God prepares us, teaches us, and gives us gifts, perhaps of faith, or the Holy Spirit interceding on our behalf, and the list can go on, that we can serve the Lord, if we recognize that still small voice and make ourselves available.

I am reminded of the story of Saul when he was supposed to wait for Samuel to come to give a sacrifice. He did not kill Agag but kept him alive. He did not eliminate all the livestock and chose to make a sacrifice before Samuel arrived. He had disobeyed the commands of the prophet who spoke for God. So sad. But Samuel's proclamation is what has always stuck with me. Saul decided he was doing good with his sacrifice. Samuel exclaimed, "Obedience is better than sacrifice." We should always do what the Lord tells us to do, but remember, He will never ask for your obedience for anything he did not prepare you for. How did He prepare you? What sacrifice do you put before obedience?

From that time on, after my time with Verna, I would look at people very different than before. Verna was a gift from God to give me a tool I could use for the rest of my life, throughout my life, in every circumstance, *if I* chose to use it. We still have our free will, and like a carpenter creating a work, he uses a variety of tools to craft what is envisioned. Sometimes the artist chooses the correct or best tool, but sometimes he looks past the right tool. God does the same with us. But He always uses the right tools for his work. Your choice, but He made it available.

The tool, the gift I was given, was a precious opportunity to look on persons and circumstances with a new set of eyes. That single point in time and that special person was the vehicle God used to make me aware of the gift He gave me so I might serve Him.

So you see, I wanted to share this point in time, about this one special person, this spirit awakening moment as a young person, that was put in my life, so that when the Lord needed me to serve Him, I would be able to see people and circumstances differently than I may have without the reminder of Verna's sacrifice. And so I was being prepared at a young age to fulfill my prayers to serve my Lord, even from a young age through my life, even to now.

I leave the reader with these thoughts: Have you taken a look back to remember if there was a time or person, a "Verna" God placed in your life? Were you given a new opportunity to get to know the living God in a personal way? Have you been given the opportunity to understand that you have been looking at this through your eyes, through our human and earthly perspective? Were you given a "Verna" to help you change your eyesight and to teach you something about the way God might want you to see His ways? And did it create in you a new heart, so maybe, just maybe, you would see through "the eyes of God"?

Tlingit Ladies

About the Author

The author is the second child of six, of a mother and father who are part of the first generation of European immigrants who fled before WWII. His good Christian parents truly were from that greatest generation. He spent his formative years in a small Alaska town, Sitka, which was the original Russian capital of Alaska. This was just after that territory became the forty-ninth state. After returning to the south forty-eight, he attended high school, graduated, and departed for the US Navy from a small rural town in Southern California during the Vietnam war era. He served his country for twenty-four years, both active and reserve, while attending college and working in the medical device development arena. He married again, a wonderful Christian woman from Orange County, California, and she supported him through those military years, college, future research companies, and teaching and political opportunities until, kind of, retirement. They have spent forty-one of their forty-two years of marriage in the same city and church family in the Inland Empire of California, where they have served and supported the church and the Lord's work where ever they could. The strength and prayers of his men's Bible study groups over the last several years also gave him the support and courage to put down in word this story he felt he should share.